BIG BAD WOLF?

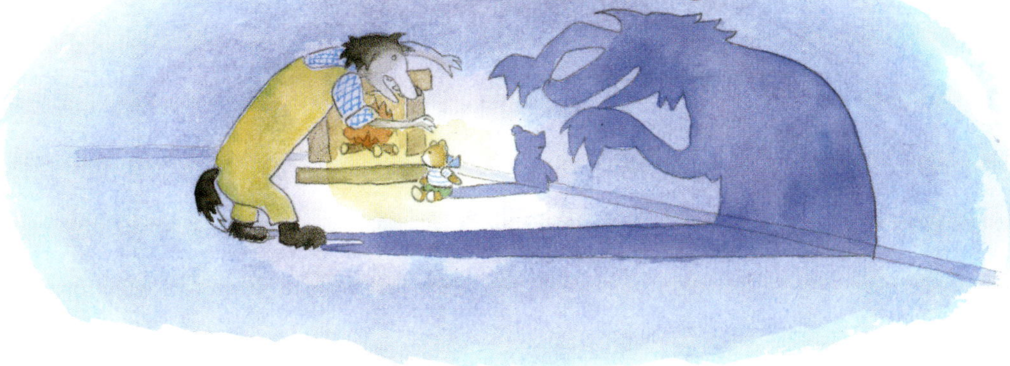

Mary Walker
Illustrated by Daniela Scarpa

RIGBY

One day Little Wolf went to visit his
uncle, Mr Wolf.
"Come in!" said Mr Wolf.

But Little Wolf said, "I'm scared you're a Big Bad Wolf.

I'm scared you will huff and **huff** and **huff** and blow everything away!"

Mr Wolf said, "Who me?
I'm as good as good can be.
I won't huff and blow everything away."

But Little Wolf said, "I'm scared you're
a Big Bad Wolf.

I'm scared you will puff and **puff**
and **puff** and blow the house down!"

Mr Wolf said, "Who me?
I'm as good as good can be.
I won't puff and blow the house down."

But Little Wolf said, "I'm scared you're
a Big Bad Wolf.

I'm scared you will growl and **growl**
and **growl** and eat everybody up!"

Mr Wolf said, "Who me?
I'm as good as good can be.
I won't growl and eat everybody up."

But Little Wolf said, "I'm scared you're a Big Bad Wolf.

I'm scared you will howl and **howl** and **howl** all night long!"

Mr Wolf said, "Who me?
I'm as good as good can be.
I won't howl all night long."

10

Then Little Wolf said, "You scare me!

I'm scared you really **are** a Big Bad Wolf."

"Don't be scared," said Mr Wolf.
"I don't like to scare.
I like my teddy bear.
Goodnight!"